Treasured Talks
Alphabet Prayers for Little Believers

Damarius Vernon

Copyright ©2024 by Damarius Vernon

All rights reserved.

No part of this book may be reproduced or transmitted in any form or by any means, electronic or mechanical, including photocopying, recording, or by any information storage and retrieval system, without permission in writing from the copyright author, except for the use of brief quotations in a book review.

ISBN: 978-1-63960-037-3 paperback

Published in the United States by Pen2Pad Ink Publishing www.pen2padink.org.

Front cover image art and interior illustrations by Arketa Williams and Pen2Pad Ink Design Studio.

Damarius Vernon retains the right to all images.

I dedicate this book to my husband, Mr. Steven Vernon, who not only believes in me but supports me in all that I do; to my daughters, Mrs. Jasmine Straughter and Janiya Vernon; and to my grandchildren, Cai, Camille, and Caileigh.

To my parents, Mr. and Mrs. Larry Lucas Sr., who ensured we were always covered in prayer and introduced us to a prayerful life at an early age.

I also dedicate this book to my siblings: Mr. Oyama Lucas and Mr. Larry Lucas Jr. (brothers), and Mrs. Nakiea Thomas (sister). To my goddaughter Bre'al Hillary and godson Jamicah Thomas, and last but not least, to my Pastor, Dr. Regina Spellmon, who believes in the power of prayer.

I dedicate this book with deep gratitude to the three prayer teams I am part of: the Monday night group, the Tuesday night group (thanks to my aunt Gwen Vernon for inviting me), and the Saturday group at Relevant Worship Center. Special thanks to the wise Charlotte Carroll, who foresaw my growth through this extraordinary journey.

To all of you who have continually prayed for me, even when I was unaware, thank you. For those who understand the dedication of prayer assignments at 2:00 and 3:00 in the morning, you are invaluable. To those of you who took the time to pause what you were doing to call and pray with me, I will be forever thankful.

Ask

Dear God,

Matthew 7:7 says, "Ask, and it will be given to you; seek, and you shall find; knock, and it will be opened to you." Lord, I ask for your presence in my life at all times, as I always seek you through the good times and bad times.

In Jesus Name,

Amen

Believe

Dear God,

Acts 16:31 says, "Believe in the Lord Jesus and you will be saved, you and your household." Lord, I believe that you were born for me, that you suffered for me, that you died for me. Help me to always believe in you no matter what.

In Jesus Name,

Amen

Confident

Dear God,

Philippians 1:6 says, "Being confident of this, that he who began a good work in you will carry it on to completion until the day of Christ Jesus." Lord, I pray that I am confident that everything you have put in me shall work in my favor.

In Jesus Name,

Amen

Determined

Dear God,

Job 14:5 says, "A person's days are determined: you have decreed the number of his months and have set limits he cannot exceed." Lord, I am determined that my beginning, my end and everything about my life is already covered.

In Jesus Name,

Amen

Effective

Dear God,

James 5:16 says, "Therefore confess your sins to each other and pray for each other so that you may be healed. The prayers of a righteous person is powerful and effective." Lord, keep my prayer life effective so my daily life will remain useful for your kingdom.

In Jesus Name,

Amen

Forgive

Dear God,

1 John 1:9 says, "If we confess our sins, He is faithful and just to forgive us our sins and to cleanse us from all unrighteousness." Lord, please help me to forgive others who wrong me as this is pleasing to you.

In Jesus Name,

Amen

Goodness

Dear God,

Psalm 23:6 says, "Surely goodness and love will follow me all the days of my life, and I will dwell in the house of the Lord forever." Lord, thank you for gifting me with your goodness every day of my life. That is your will and so shall it be.

In Jesus Name,

Amen

Heaven

Dear God,

Philippians 3:20-21 says, "But our citizenship is in heaven, and from it we await a Savior, the Lord Jesus Christ, who will transform our lowly body to be like his glorious body, by the power that enables him even to subject all things to himself." Lord, although I am in this world it is not my home, it is my assignment. Thank you for preparing the best home for me.

In Jesus Name,

Amen

Inherit

Dear God,

Psalm 37:9 says, "For those who are evil will be destroyed, but those who hope in the Lord will inherit the land." Lord, my hope is in you and you alone, and because of this I will inherit the land. Let your will be done.

In Jesus Name,

Amen

Joy

Dear God,

John 15:11 says, "These things have I spoken unto you, that my joy might remain in you, and that your joy might be filled." Lord, thank you for giving me unspeakable joy throughout my day, as I remain in you.

In Jesus Name,

Amen

Keeper

Dear God,

Proverbs 1:7 says, "The fear of the Lord is the beginning of knowledge; fools despise wisdom and instruction." Lord, the fear I have for you is not pleasing you, as you are great in all your ways. Keep me wanting wisdom from you and you alone.

In Jesus Name,

Amen

Love

Dear God,

1 Corinthians 16:14 says, "Let all that you do be done in love." Lord, I want to show love in everything that I do, the same way you show your love towards me.

In Jesus Name,

Amen

Mountain

Dear God,

Matthew 17:20 says, He replied, "Because you have so little faith. Truly I tell you, if you have faith as small as a mustard seed, you can say to this mountain, 'Move from here to there,' and it will move. Nothing will be impossible for you." Lord, every mountain that shows up in my life that does not line up with your will, it shall be removed because of my faith.

In Jesus Name,

Amen

Needs

Dear God,

Philippians 4:19 says, "And my God will meet all of your needs according to the riches of his glory in Christ Jesus." Lord, you know where I am in life at all times. Thank you for supplying all my needs according to your will and not mine.

In Jesus Name,

Amen

Obey

Dear God,

Ephesians 6:1 says, "Children, obey your parents in the Lord for this is right." Lord, help me to always honor my parents and to always obey them. I pray my parents seek you for guidance for this is right in your sight.

In Jesus Name,

Amen

Peace

Dear God,

Numbers 6:24-26 says, "The Lord bless you and keep you; the Lord make his face shine on you and be gracious to you; the Lord turn his face toward you and give you peace." Lord, I thank you for the peace that you give me. Allow me to always be in the presence of your peace.

In Jesus Name,

Amen

Quickening

Dear God,

Psalm 71:20 (NLT) says, "You have allowed me to suffer much hardship, but you will restore me to life again and lift me up from the depths of the earth." Lord, may your favor come quickly to restore me in my times of trouble.

In Jesus Name,

Amen

Renew

Dear God,

Psalm 51:10 says, "Create in me a clean heart O God and renew a right spirit within me." Lord, cleanse my heart daily so that my spirit is presented right to you.

In Jesus Name,

Amen

Spirit

Dear God,

John 4:24 says, "God is spirit, and they that worship him must worship him in spirit and in truth." Lord, my worship belongs to only you. I speak that I shall always worship you in spirit and truth.

In Jesus Name,

Amen

Trust

Dear God,

Proverbs 3:5 says, "Trust in the Lord with all your heart and lean not to your own understanding." Lord, help me to trust you in all things I do not understand. I shall put all my trust in you, as you are my creator and the creator of all things.

In Jesus Name,

Amen

Understanding

Dear God,

1 John 5:20 says, "We know also that the Son of God has come and has given us understanding so that we may know Him who is true." Lord, continue to give us understanding to always know you and you alone.

In Jesus Name,

Amen

Victory

Dear God,

1 John 5:4 says, "For everyone born of God overcome the world. This is the victory that has overcome the world, even our faith." Lord, I ask for your presence in my life as I always seek you through both good and bad times.

Psalm 20:6 says, "Now this I know the Lord gives victory to His anointed." Lord, keep my anointing fresh so that I may always find victory in you.

In Jesus Name,

Amen

Wisdom

Dear God,

Proverbs 3:13 says, "Blessed are those who find wisdom, those who gain understanding." Lord, to have wisdom is to understand you. Help me to remain blessed because of your wisdom.

In Jesus Name,

Amen

Xerxes

Dear God,

Ester 1:19 says, "Therefore, if it pleases the king, let him issue a royal decree and let it be written in the laws of Persia and Media, which cannot be repealed, that Vashti is never again to enter the presence of King Xerxes." Lord, allow me to find favor in any place that I enter.

In Jesus Name,

Amen

Yoke

Dear God,

Matthew 11:29 says, "Take my yoke upon you and learn of me, for I am meek and lowly in heart, and ye shall find rest unto your souls." Lord, help me to depend on you and trust in you. Giving you complete control to direct my life.

In Jesus Name,

Amen

Zion

Dear God,

Psalm 132:13 says, "For the Lord hath chosen Zion, he hath desired it for his habitation." Lord, you are the Lord of Zion. All my praises belong to you as I come before your throne. It is your glory I seek.

In Jesus Name,

Amen